LEBRON JAMES

Making a Difference as a Sports Superstar

By Katie Kawa

People Who Make a Difference

Published in 2022 by
KidHaven Publishing, an Imprint of Greenhaven Publishing, LLC
29 E. 21st Street
New York, NY 10010

Designer: Deanna Paternostro
Editor: Katie Kawa

Photo credits: Cover Thearon W. Henderson/Getty Images Sport/Getty Images; p. 5 Marco Secchi/Getty Images Sport/Getty Images; p. 7 Lucy Nicholson/Stringer/AFP/Getty Images; p. 9 Scott Meivogel/Shutterstock.com; p. 11 Miami Herald/Tribune News Service/Getty Images; p. 13 MediaNews Group/Bay Area News via Getty Images/MediaNews Group/Getty Images; p. 15 Allison Farrand/Contributor/National Basketball Association/Getty Images; p. 17 Joe Robbins/Stringer/Getty Images Sport/Gett Images; p. 18 Justin Sullivan/Staff/Getty Images News/Getty Images; p. 20 Antonio Scorza/Staff/AFP/Getty Images; p. 21 T.Sumaetho/Shutterstock.com.

Library of Congress Cataloging-in-Publication Data

Names: Kawa, Katie, author.
Title: LeBron James : making a difference as a sports superstar / Katie Kawa.
Description: New York : KidHaven Publishing, 2022. | Series: People who make a difference | Includes index.
Identifiers: LCCN 2020032838 | ISBN 9781534536876 (library binding) | ISBN 9781534536852 (paperback) | ISBN 9781534536869 (set) | ISBN 9781534536883 (ebook)
Subjects: LCSH: James, LeBron–Juvenile literature. | Basketball players–United States–Biography–Juvenile literature. | African American basketball players–Biography–Juvenile literature.
Classification: LCC GV884.J36 K38 2022 | DDC 796.323092 [B]–dc23
LC record available at https://lccn.loc.gov/2020032838

Printed in the United States of America

CPSIA compliance information: Batch #CW22KH: For further information contact Greenhaven Publishing LLC, New York, New York at 1-844-317-7404.

Please visit our website, www.greenhavenpublishing.com. For a free color catalog of all our high-quality books, call toll free 1-844-317-7404 or fax 1-844-317-7405.

CONTENTS

A LEADER ON AND OFF THE COURT

LeBron James is a leader on the basketball court. In fact, he's often known as King James. He's led his teams to big wins in the National Basketball Association (NBA). He's won NBA **championships** and Olympic gold **medals**. When kids around the world play basketball with their friends, they want to be like LeBron.

LeBron knows that kids want to be like him, and he tries to set a good example for them. He does this by speaking out about issues that matter to him and working hard to make a difference in his community. LeBron is leader off the basketball court too!

In His Words

"I have so many kids, and … adults … looking for someone to kind of lead them in times where they feel like their voice isn't powerful … And when you see something that's unjust or you see something that's wrong or you see something that's trying to **divide** us as a race or as a country, then I feel like my voice can be heard."

— Interview with ESPN from July 2018

LeBron James knows it's just as important to make a difference off the court as it is to make a difference on it.

HARD TIMES

LeBron James was born in Akron, Ohio, on December 30, 1984. LeBron didn't have an easy childhood. Gloria James was only 16 when she gave birth to LeBron, and LeBron's father wasn't a part of his life. LeBron's grandmother helped Gloria, but after she died, Gloria was on her own.

Gloria and LeBron sometimes lived with her friends or family members because they didn't have a home of their own. LeBron often missed school because he was moving from place to place. However, his life changed when he started playing sports, especially football. Playing sports helped LeBron learn to believe in himself.

In His Words

"There's no way [I] should've made it out, but the word 'sport' … saved my life."

— Interview on the "Road Trippin'" **podcast** from March 2017

Gloria James wanted to give LeBron his best chance to succeed. She let him live with Frank Walker—a football coach—and his family so LeBron could have a better life. The Walkers made sure LeBron went to school, and they signed him up to play on a basketball team.

HIGH SCHOOL SUPERSTAR

LeBron was a talented football player and basketball player when he was growing up. In fact, he played both sports at St. Vincent-St. Mary High School in Akron. He eventually chose basketball as the sport he wanted to keep playing in the future.

LeBron won three state championships as a basketball player in high school. He became famous for his skills on the court. While he was still in high school, he was on the cover of *Sports Illustrated*—a popular sports magazine. LeBron decided to start playing in the NBA right after high school. He started his NBA **career** with the Cleveland Cavaliers in 2003.

In His Words

"The spotlight hasn't messed me up … I chose this life, and there's no way I'm trying to get away from it."

— Story printed in the *Pittsburgh Post-Gazette* newspaper in December 2002

LeBron was excited to play for the Cavaliers. Cleveland, Ohio, isn't far from Akron, so he was able to start his NBA career close to home.

MAKING THE DECISION

LeBron didn't waste any time becoming one of the best players in the NBA. In 2004, he was named the NBA Rookie of the Year—the player who was the most successful in his first year. LeBron led the Cavaliers to the NBA **playoffs** multiple times. He was also named the NBA's Most Valuable Player (MVP) twice while playing in Cleveland in the early part of his career.

However, LeBron wanted to win a championship, and it seemed like it would be hard to do that in Cleveland. In 2010, LeBron announced that he was going to play for the Miami Heat. He won two championships with the Heat, in 2012 and 2013.

In His Words

"You … have to live with your decision that you're going to make, and you have to do what's best for you, for your family, and for you to … be happy."

— "The Decision," which was the 2010 EPSN TV special in which LeBron announced he was going to Miami

One big reason LeBron went to play in Miami, Florida, was because he wanted to play with Chris Bosh (left) and Dwyane Wade (center). The three of them were very successful as teammates!

A HOMETOWN HERO

LeBron finally knew what it felt like to be a champion. Next, he wanted his hometown to know how that felt too. In 2014, he returned to Cleveland with one goal: to win a championship in Ohio. The Cavaliers had never won a championship, and the city of Cleveland had gone 52 years without any of its major sports teams winning one.

In 2016, LeBron finally brought a championship to Cleveland when the Cavaliers beat the Golden State Warriors in Game 7 of the NBA Finals. LeBron was named the MVP of the Finals that year—a title he also earned twice in Miami.

In His Words

"I feel my calling here goes above basketball. I have a **responsibility** to lead, in more ways than one, and I take that very **seriously**. My presence can make a difference in Miami, but I think it can mean more where I'm from."

— Story written for *Sports Illustrated* in July 2014

LeBron knew how much winning a championship meant to the city of Cleveland and all the surrounding parts of Ohio, including his hometown of Akron. He was happy to give these cities something to be proud of.

I PROMISE

LeBron came back to the Cavaliers because he wanted to make a lasting difference in the state where he grew up. He knew that was going to take more than just winning a championship.

LeBron started the LeBron James Family Foundation in 2004 to help kids in Akron. This foundation runs the I Promise program, which provides **mentors** and other help to kids growing up in **situations** that could make it harder for them to succeed. In 2018, LeBron helped these kids even more when he opened the I Promise School. This public school gives kids and their parents tools to succeed.

In His Words

"For me to be able to be in a position where I can give these kids options to decide what they want to do with their future, it's probably the best thing I've ever done."

— Interview with CNN about the I Promise School from February 2020

LeBron is shown here at the opening of the I Promise School. This school provides free meals and uniforms for students and helps parents finish their education and find a job. In addition, its students can go to college for free!

TAKING THE FAMILY TO CALIFORNIA

The LeBron James Family Foundation and the I Promise School have continued to help the people of Akron even after LeBron moved to California in 2018. That year, he signed a contract to play with the Los Angeles Lakers. In 2020, he won a championship with the Lakers.

LeBron has done more than just play basketball in California. He's made movies too! In 2021, LeBron starred in *Space Jam: A New Legacy*. LeBron made a family movie because family is important to him. He married his high school sweetheart, Savannah. As of 2021, they have three children: LeBron Jr. (often called Bronny), Bryce, and Zhuri.

In His Words

"What really helped me out, becoming a parent, is what I went through as a kid, not having a dad … I wanted to have kids early, to prove to my father that the way you did it was the absolute wrong way to do it, and I wanted to break the mold to where I want to be there and give them all the life skills."

— Interview for the Uninterrupted YouTube channel from 2018

LeBron wants to be the best dad he can be. He's shown here with Savannah at one of Bronny's basketball games in 2019.

RAISING AWARENESS

LeBron is one of the most famous **athletes** in the world. When he talks, people listen. He tries to use this power for good. LeBron has given speeches and has talked openly about issues that mean a lot to him. He also uses social media platforms, such as Twitter and Instagram, to help call attention to problems in the world.

LeBron has been very active in the fight against **racism** in the United States. He's helped raise awareness about the problem of police **violence** against Black Americans. He's also started the group More Than a Vote to help Black Americans exercise their right to vote.

In His Words

"Change doesn't happen sitting on the sideline."

— Tweet from June 2020

The Life of LeBron James

1984
LeBron James is born on December 30.

2003
LeBron begins playing in the NBA with the Cleveland Cavaliers.

2004
LeBron is named Rookie of the Year and starts the LeBron James Family Foundation.

2008
LeBron wins an Olympic gold medal.

2012
LeBron wins his first NBA championship with the Miami Heat and his second Olympic gold medal.

2013
LeBron wins a second NBA championship with the Heat.

2016
LeBron leads the Cavaliers to their first NBA championship.

2018
LeBron opens the I Promise School and joins the Los Angeles Lakers.

2020
LeBron wins his first NBA championship as a Laker and starts More Than a Vote.

2021
LeBron stars in the movie *Space Jam: A New Legacy.*

LeBron's life has featured many big moments on and off the basketball court.

BIGGER THAN BASKETBALL

Many people believe LeBron James is one of the best basketball players ever. He's a superstar in the United States and around the world. At the 2008 and 2012 Olympic Games, LeBron was part of U.S. teams that won gold medals playing against teams from other countries.

Some people say that LeBron and other athletes should stick to playing sports and not talk about problems in the world, such as racism. However, LeBron knows those people are wrong. He's making a difference not just by talking about problems, but also by working to fix them.

In His Words

"I get to sit up here and talk about what's really important ... I will definitely not [stop talking] ... I mean too much to so many kids that feel like they don't have a way out and they need someone to help lead them out of the situation they're in ... This is bigger than me playing the game of basketball."

— Interview during NBA All-Star Weekend in February 2018

Be Like LeBron James!

Find ways to help your community—from cleaning up a park to collecting food for families who are hungry.

Stand up for what you know is right and for people who aren't being treated fairly.

Work hard in school.

Be a team player who helps others succeed.

Raise money for groups that help kids in need.

Find a sport or other activity you like, and practice to get better at it.

Learn more about important issues, such as racism. Ask questions and read books to educate yourself.

LeBron knows not to listen to people who tell him he can't make a difference in the world around him. These are some ways you can be like him and make a difference in the world around you!

GLOSSARY

athlete: A person who plays a sport.

career: A period of time spent doing a job or activity.

championship: A contest to find out who's the best player or team in a sport.

divide: To separate into different groups.

medal: A flat, small piece of metal with art or words that's used as an honor or reward.

mentor: A person who teaches, gives guidance, or gives advice to someone, especially a less experienced person.

playoffs: A series of games played after the regular season of a sport is over to find out who the best team is that season.

podcast: A show that people can use the internet to listen to that often features people talking about a certain topic or interviewing famous people.

racism: The practice of treating others poorly because they are part of a different race, or group of people who look alike in certain ways. This word also relates to governments and societies that allow one race to be treated better than others.

responsibility: A duty that a person should do.

seriously: Done with care.

situation: All the facts, conditions, and events that affect someone or something in a certain time and place.

violence: The use of force to harm someone.

FOR MORE INFORMATION

WEBSITES

ESPN: LeBron James

www.espn.com/nba/player/_/id/1966/lebron-james

LeBron's ESPN page has videos, news articles, and important facts about the games he's played in.

LeBron James Family Foundation

www.lebronjamesfamilyfoundation.org/

The official website of the LeBron James Family Foundation has stories and videos about the foundation and the I Promise School.

BOOKS

Hewson, Anthony K. *LeBron James*. Minnetonka, MN: Kaleidoscope Publishing, 2020.

Santos, Rita. *LeBron James: Basketball Superstar*. New York, NY: Enslow Publishing, 2020.

Steele, Laura Price. *LeBron James*. North Mankato, MN: Capstone Press, 2020.

INDEX